"A friend loveth at all times." Proverbs 17:17

"Love never fails." 1 Corinthians 13:8

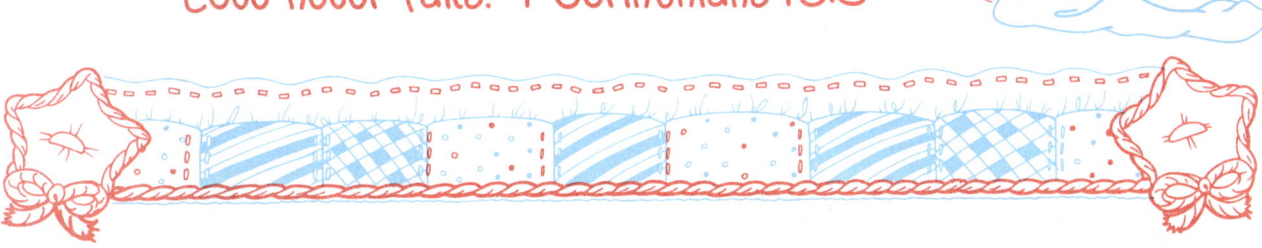

"Be kind to one another." Ephesians 4:32

"Do not be afraid." John 14:27

"A friend loveth at all times." Proverbs 17:17

"Love never fails." 1 Corinthians 13:8

"Do not be afraid." John 14:27

"A friend loveth at all times." Proverbs 17:17

"Love never fails." 1 Corinthians 13:8

"Be kind to one another." Ephesians 4:32

"A friend loveth at all times." Proverbs 17:17

"Love never fails." 1 Corinthians 13:8

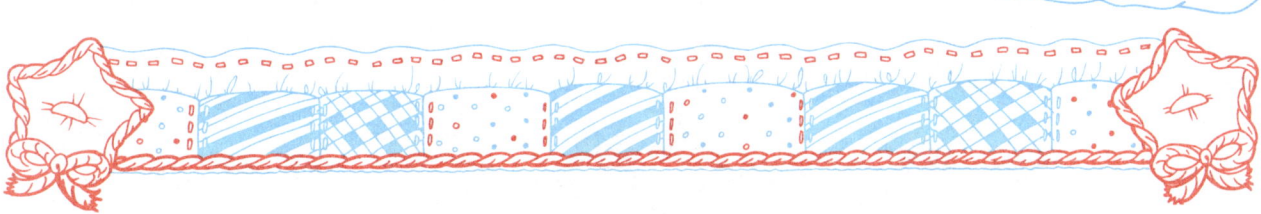

"Be kind to one another." Ephesians 4:32

"Do not be afraid." John 14:27

"A friend loveth at all times." Proverbs 17:17

"Love never fails." 1 Corinthians 13:8

"Do not be afraid." John 14:27

"A friend loveth at all times." Proverbs 17:17

"Love never fails." 1 Corinthians 13:8

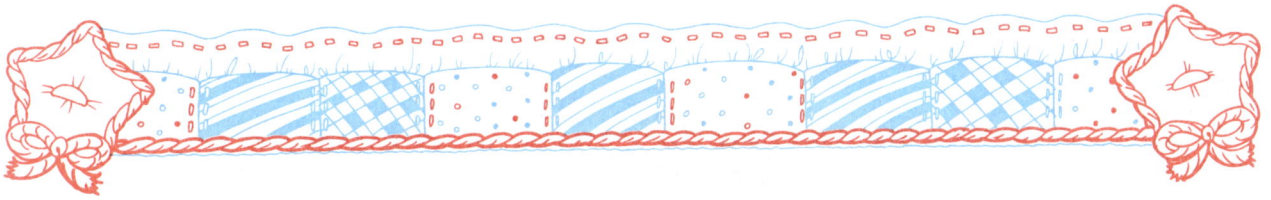

"Do not be afraid." John 14:27

"A friend loveth at all times." Proverbs 17:17

"Love never fails." 1 Corinthians 13:8

"Do not be afraid." John 14:27

"A friend loveth at all times." Proverbs 17:17

"Love never fails." 1 Corinthians 13:8

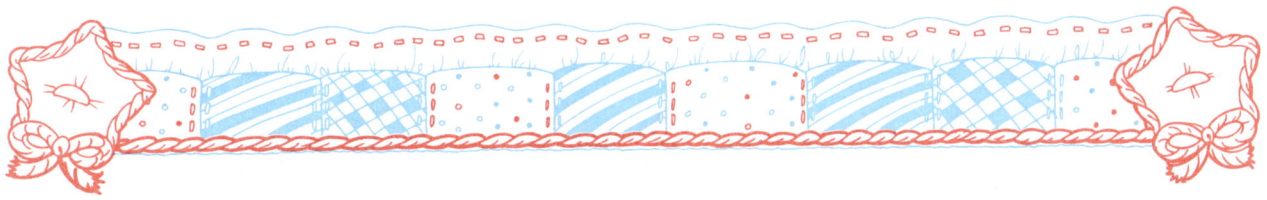